TOTALLY WEIRD

Natural Disasters

Contents

Ouch!

Tricky words are explained on page 32.

Nature's

Natural disasters are massive catastrophes that strike the world from time to time. Disasters can be caused by ferocious weather or by powerful movements inside the Earth. Some even come from space!

wild

A big, fiery cauldron

The Earth is covered with plates of solid rock that float on a sea of boiling hot, melted rock, called magma. Most of the time the plates float peacefully, but...

solid rock

magma

Disasters are deadly

Natural disasters are amazing to see but don't forget that often the kill many people. Experts try to gi warnings before disasters happen but sometimes there's no time to escape. Then, teams of rescuers rush to the scene to provide food, shelter and medical help.

Hot shots

...when the plates move apart or slide under each other, the fiery magma bubbles up between the plates and explodes on to the Earth's surface.

Cracking up

When the plates grind against each other with a shudder, the ground shakes and buildings crumble. An earthquake has begun!

▲ This tangled wreckage was once a row of houses. During a terrible storm, fierce winds tore the buildings apart.

Exploding volcanoes

Volcanoes are packed full of liquid rock called lava. Some volcanoes spurt out fountains of lava every day. Others sleep for thousands of years, then wake with a huge explosion. This super-charged bang can rip the volcano apart!

Return of the Ice age

In the 1500s, two massive volcanoes erupted. They shot enormous clouds of ash into the sky, which blocked out the sun. Europe turned icy cold and the Arctic Ocean froze over. Polar bears could have trekked across the frozen sea to visit new lands!

THE SLEEPING GIANT AWAKES

1. Mount St. Helens volcano in Washington State, USA, lay asleep for 123 years. Then, in 1980, its sides began to bulge slowly outwards.

2. Suddenly, the volcano blew its top. Scorching ash and clouds of gas flew into the air. Nearby streams became so hot that fish leapt out of the water!

3. Snow on the sides of the volcano melted in seconds and mixed with the ash, creating monster mud flows that destroyed more than 200 homes.

4. Luckily, scientists had warned people living near the volcano that the blast was about to happen. Thousands were able to flee to safety.

...and **rivers** of **fire!**

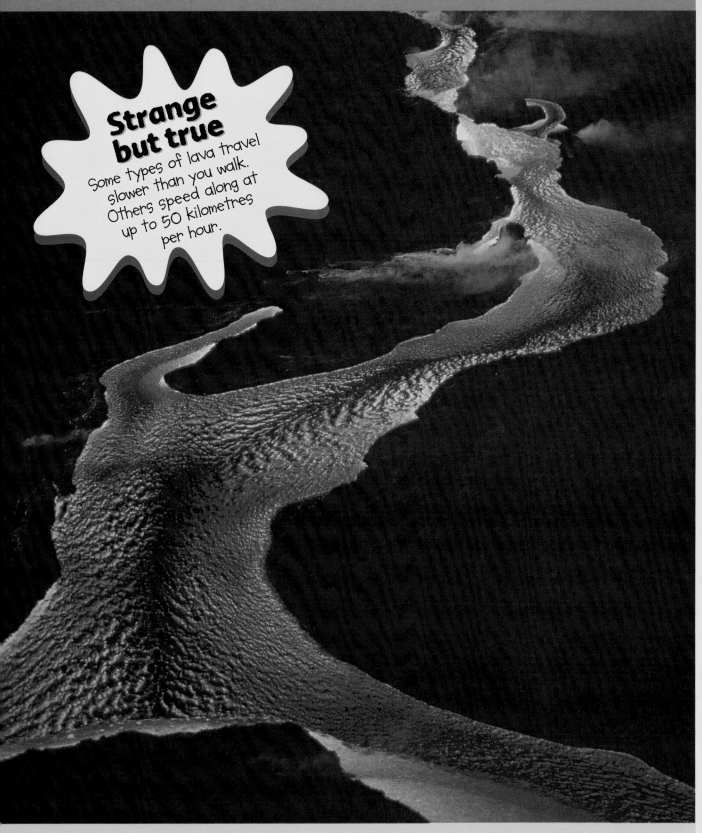

Strange but true

Some types of lava travel slower than you walk. Others speed along at up to 50 kilometres per hour.

▲ A fiery river of lava oozes down the slopes of this volcano in Hawaii, USA, burning everything in its path. When the lava cools, it covers the land in a blanket of solid, grey rock.

Cast in stone

After a volcano erupts, things are never quite the same. When the hot lava and ash cool, they turn into hard rocks. Many of these rocks have weird shapes. Others hide incredible secrets.

Homes in cones

These fairy-tale cones were left by volcanoes that erupted eight million years ago in Turkey. Rain washed away the softer parts of the cones to form caves where people made their homes. A few people still live here today.

Smothered in ash

In AD 79, in Italy, a giant volcano called Mount Vesuvius erupted. It showered the Roman town of Pompeii with scorching ash. People tried to flee but they were all buried alive. Over time, the ash turned to rock, trappi the unlucky victims forever in stone tombs.

DISCOVERING THE PEOPLE OF POMPEII

1 Centuries later, archaeologists dug into the rock at Pompeii and discovered holes in the shape of people. The bodies in the holes had rotted away a long time ago.

2 The archaeologists used the holes as moulds. They poured in runny plaster of Paris and waited for it to set.

3 When the plaster was dry, the archaeologists chipped away the surrounding rock. They were left with plaster models of the fleeing Romans and their pets!

▲ This photograph of plaster-cast people from Pompeii shows how the force of the blast knocked everyone to the ground. It captures a gruesome scene frozen in time.

On the move

CRACK!

That's weird

In 1995, an earthquake devastated Kobe, Japan, but the airport survived without a scratch. It was resting on huge spongy feet which acted like giant cushions. The airport simply rode out the shakes.

When the Earth's plates rub each other the wrong way, the ground jumps and rattles, causing an earthquake. Most earthquakes are so small that people don't notice them. But a large earthquake can destroy cities and even move mountains!

Making waves

Earthquakes under the sea create the biggest waves in the world, called tsunamis. When a tsunami hits the coast, the massive wave can travel twice as fast as a racing car and may be three times higher than a house. It swallows everything in its path and then sucks it back out to sea.

The Great San Francisco Fire

In 1906, an earthquake hit San Francisco, USA, causing a double disaster. First, many buildings toppled over. Then, broken gas pipes, electricity wires and cookers sparked off fires that burned down most of the city.

To the rescue

After an earthquake, the race is on to find people trapped in the rubble. Specially trained dogs with super-sensitive noses sniff their way towards a survivor. Then they bark the good news to a rescue team which pulls the person to safety.

▲ A major earthquake is over in a few seconds, but it can reduce a town to rubble.

Wild winds

Hurricanes are fierce storms that set off the world's wildest winds. Out at sea, hurricane winds can whip up monster waves that sink ships. On land, they can rip up trees and blow down houses.

▲ In 1992, a mighty hurricane, named Andrew, battered the coast of Florida, USA. Winds raced along at 280 kilometres per hour, flinging boats on to the streets!

All in a spin

This photograph, taken from space, shows a hurricane spinning across the ocean towards the USA. The most dangerous winds and the heaviest rains lurk in the thick, white part of the storm.

Sneaky storm

The centre of a hurricane, called the eye, is completely still. When the eye passes over, everything is calm. You think the storm's finished, but really you're right in the middle of it. Spooky!

What's in a name?

Every hurricane has a name to make it easy to identify. The first person to label hurricanes was a weather forecaster who lived in the 1800s. He named them after people he didn't like!

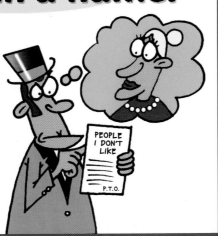

PEOPLE
I DON'T
LIKE

P.T.O.

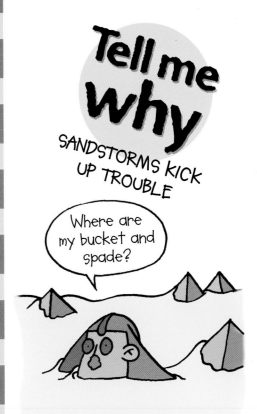

Where are my bucket and spade?

In Egypt, strong winds fly across the desert and whip up wicked sandstorms called haboobs. The winds can smother whole villages and even the ancient pyramids, in clouds of sand and dust.

Millions of years ago, scary sandstorms raged through the Gobi Desert in Asia, burying dinosaurs and their eggs. The hot sand kept the eggs perfectly preserved. So now, it's a top spot for dino-experts!

Terrible twister

A tornado, or twister, is a deadly tube of wind that snakes down from the sky. When it hits the ground, it sucks up everything in its path like a monster-sized vacuum cleaner. A really powerful twister can even toss train carriages into the air.

Must be mad...

When most people see a twister, they run quickly in the opposite direction, but storm chasers don't. They spend their time in hot pursuit of twisters. Filming a pair of twisters, called sisters, would really make their day!

Touchdown

This deadly twister formed from storm clouds in Monument Valley in Arizona, USA. When a twister hits the ground, it makes a deafening roar and dust shoots everywhere. It then spins along on a journey of destruction.

Lucky escape

In 1986, in China, a tornado picked up 13 school children and carried them through the air for 19 kilometres. When it put them down again, they were completely unharmed!

12

Strange but true

A waterspout can suck up fish as it moves across the water. When the spout stops spinning, the fish rain down on people's heads.

▲ When a tornado forms over the sea or a lake, it whips up the surface of the water into a tall, spinning column, called a waterspout.

Flood alert

Rain is the all-time biggest cause of natural disasters. Short downpours flood houses in a flash and non-stop rain makes rivers swell until they burst, spreading millions of litres of muddy water across the land.

That's weird

Floods even happen in deserts. When a storm breaks out in nearby hills, water races down the slopes. Then, it surges along channels in the dry desert, sweeping up everything in its path.

THE GREAT FLOOD

The Bible tells how, long ago, God decided to send a mighty flood to punish all the bad people in the world. He told a man named Noah to build a boat called an ark. God wanted to save Noah's family and two of every kind of animal.

The rain fell for 40 days and 40 nights. The flood rose so high, it covered the highest mountains. But Noah's ark floated safely.

At last, the waters dropped and the ark landed on a mountain top. Noah and the animals began a new life and God promised never to send another flood like it again.

Holy cow!

Often, the only way for people to escape a major flood is by helicopter – and animals are not forgotten, either! A helicopter picks up stranded cows and sheep. The confused creatures are put in a harness and carried up, up and away.

High and dry

In some hot countries, many people live high up off the ground in houses built on stilts. These people know that every year during the rainy season, rain pours non-stop for days on end. While towns and villages flood, these clever clogs stay safe and dry in their high-rise homes.

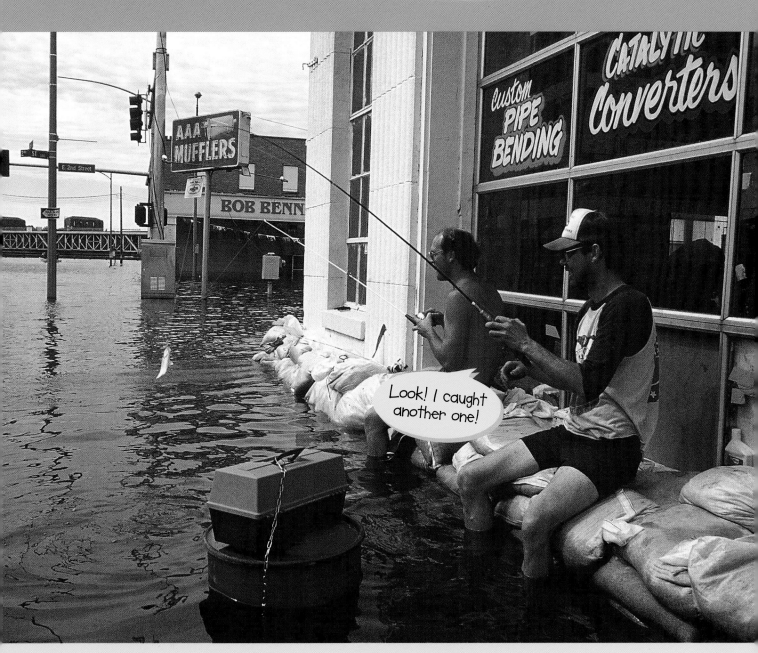

▲ These men are fishing in the road during a flood. They could be here for quite a while – flood water can take weeks to drain away completely.

White out

Wicked winter weather brings extra-special dangers. Wild snowstorms trap people in their homes. Scarier still, mighty avalanches charge down mountain slopes. These giant snowslides bury everything in their path.

Monster drifts

Blizzards are a deadly duo of heavy snowfall and strong winds. The bone-chilling blasts quickly drive snow into massive piles, called drifts. The most dastardly drifts grow three or four times higher than an adult. That's tall enough to bury a house.

Avalanche alert!

A snowstorm is a recipe for an avalanche. When snow on a mountainside grows too heavy, it suddenly falls away. As the icy load tumbles downhill, it picks up speed, and more snow, until millions of tonnes of snow roar along. In a race with a car whizzing by at 100 kilometres per hour, an avalanche would win.

Now, where's my house?

▲ It's almost impossible to walk or even to see in a blizzard. Fierce winds blast snow around until everything is a white blur.

During World War I, avalanches were used as weapons. Soldiers fighting in the mountains in France fired guns at snowy ledges above their enemy's camp. The shots triggered avalanches that buried the enemy soldiers in snow.

Today, experts fire special guns at snow above mountain villages to protect the people who live there. The small explosions set off harmless mini-avalanches. This stops the snow from building up and setting off a huge, killer avalanche.

A dry spell

A drought is a long stretch of hot, dry weather that may go on for months or years. During a serious drought, streams dry up and green fields turn to dusty deserts.

Thirsty work

Day after day of scorching heat bakes the earth so hard that it cracks. Cattle kick up dust as they stampede across the bone-dry ground looking for food and water. Often they trek for hundreds of miles before coming across a water hole.

A BIG BOWL OF DUST

In the 1930s, a drought hit the Midwest, USA. It barely rained for 10 years! All the farmers' crops died because there was no water.

Then the ground became dry and dusty. Winds blew the dust into blinding clouds that blocked out the sun and choked the birds.

Millions of people abandoned their homes. They left a string of empty ghost towns that stretched all the way from Texas, USA, to Canada.

Beating the heat

A few places are struck by droughts again and again. When this happens, it's best to go to the source of the problem. People take to the skies in special aeroplanes. Their mission? To fire chemicals at the clouds which force out reluctant raindrops.

▲ Forest trees and bushes become hot and dry during a drought. The tiniest spark can set off a raging fire that may blaze for days, or even weeks.

Threats from outer

Thousands of rocks, called asteroids, whizz through space. Most of the time, they circle the Sun, but now and again they head straight for us. Big collisions are rare, but when they happen, they're truly earth-shattering!

▲ Asteroids come in different shapes and sizes. They can be as small as a pebble or almost as big as a planet. The largest asteroids can be hundreds of kilometres across.

Lucky escape

In 1996, an asteroid missed Earth by only 450,000 kilometres. It came as close to us as the Moon. That might sound like a long distance but, in space terms, it's a bit too close for comfort!

Dino-disaster

Many scientists blame an enormous asteroid for wiping out the dinosaurs 65 million years ago. They believe that when the rock crashed, the explosion threw up a dust cloud that blocked out the sun's rays. Earth became so dark and cold that all the dinosaurs died out.

space

Space invader

About 22,000 years ago, a massive meteorite crash-landed in the Arizona Desert, USA. It created this enormous crater. You could lay three Empire State Buildings end-to-end across the crater.

Every day, Earth is bombarded by tiny space rocks. Luckily for us, most of them burn up in the atmosphere and become shooting stars. On a clear night, you can see these 'stars' as streaks of light shooting across the sky.

Ouch!

The Moon has no atmosphere to protect it from falling space rocks, so it gets a real hammering. Its surface is dotted with as many as three billion craters!

21

Disaster

scientists

Check out these disaster scientists and their amazing disaster-detecting gadgets. These hot shots are just looking for trouble! They can't stop storms or earthquakes, but they can try to warn people in time.

THE WEATHER WATCHERS
Meteorologists work in weather centres, where they gather all kinds of information about dangerous weather. They watch how weather changes and see where it's heading.

Satellites high above Earth beam back pictures of clouds.

Crews on ships and in aeroplanes send in weather reports from faraway places.

Radar picks up signs of rain.

Volcano doctors

Vulcanologists are a bit like doctors. They have the steamy job of studying volcanoes. First, they check a volcano's sides to see if they are bulging with bubbling magma. Then, the hot docs prod the volcano with a gas detector, looking for tell-tale signs of escaping gases.

Inside the weather centre, super-fast computers make sense of all this information.

Creepy shakes

It's difficult to tell when an earthquake will happen or how big it will be. A clever machine, called a creepmetre, helps scientists predict earthquakes. It picks up tiny shivers in the ground which could mean that something much bigger is on the way.

That's weird

Often animals give the first warning of an earthquake. Worms, snakes, rats and mice have been known to scramble out of their holes just before the rumbles start.

▲ These scientists are launching a giant weather balloon. The controls on board will measure what's happening in the clouds.

Fantastic tales

Long ago, people blamed nature's terrifying powers on monsters or angry gods, and told incredible stories about their dastardly deeds. Natural events are no longer a mystery, but they make for action-packed films!

That's weird

Long ago, in Mexico, the Aztecs believed that a god lived inside the violent volcano above their city. Often, they threw young girls into the volcano, hoping that these gruesome gifts would stop the god from blowing the volcano's top.

FISH IN A FLAP

In ancient Japan, people believed that earthquakes were caused by a giant catfish that lived underground. When it wriggled in the mud, the ground shook so much that a quake began.

The gods tried to keep the flapping fish out of trouble. They pinned it down under a heavy rock so that it couldn't move.

Then, one day, a massive quake destroyed the ancient city of Edo. People believed that the catfish had wriggled free while the gods were away.

Mischievous mouse

The Native American Chippewa people of Ohio have a tale to explain floods – they blame them on a mouse! In their story, the sun's heat is stored in a bag. The peckish mouse nibbles a hole in the corner of the bag and the heat leaks out. The escaping warmth melts all the mountain snow, which floods the land.

The lost world

The ancient Greeks thought that their god, Zeus, started earthquakes when he lost his temper. One story tells how Zeus flew into a rage with the people of a magical island called Atlantis. He sent a quake that sank their island without a trace. Today, a few people still wonder if this land ever really existed.

An Event...

EARTHQUAKE

When in Southern California visit UNIVERSAL STUDIOS TOUR

...ring ...ARLTON HESTON
... GARDNER • GEORGE KENNEDY
...RNE GREENE • GENEVIEVE BUJOLD • RICHARD ROUNDTREE
...arring MARJOE GORTNER • BARRY SULLIVAN • LLOYD NOLAN • VICTORIA PRINCIPAL
...en by GEORGE FOX and MARIO PUZO Music by JOHN WILLIAMS Produced and Directed by MARK ROBSON
...utive Producer JENNINGS LANG • A MARK ROBSON-FILMAKERS GROUP PRODUCTION

ORIGINAL SOUNDTRACK AVAILABLE ON MCA RECORDS & TAPES
A UNIVERSAL PICTURE • TECHNICOLOR® PANAVISION®

PG PARENTAL GUIDANCE SUGGESTED

▲ *Earthquake* shows Los Angeles, USA, in the grip of a huge quake. When the film was first shown, a clever device in the cinema seats shook the audience so they felt they were part of the action!

There may be trOuble

It's a fact — the world is overheating. Every day, humans blast out hot, polluting fumes into the delicate atmosphere above the Earth. No one really knows what will happen next or if new kinds of natural disasters lie ahead.

Believe it or not

A few scientists think that the Earth is heating up naturally. The fumes that we release into the air just make it happen more quickly.

That's weird

When cows burp, they give off huge amounts of a world-warming gas called methane!

Turning up the heat

Planet Earth is kept cosy and warm by a special layer of gases in the atmosphere that traps some of the sun's heat. Without this layer, Earth would be deathly cold. But cars and factories pump out heat-trapping gases such as carbon dioxide, which means that too much heat is being kept in!

There is too much carbon dioxide reaching the atmosphere.

When factories and cars burn fuel, they release carbon dioxide.

ahead

Meltdown

A few scientists believe that in the future, the world could be so warm that the gigantic sheets of ice that cover the North and South Poles will melt. Huge amounts of melting ice will flood into the world's oceans. Low-lying shores will flood and islands in many parts of the world will disappear completely.

Hurricane city!

A warmed-up world could also mean more raging storms than ever before! Baby storm clouds love to feed off the steamy air that rises from warm water. It gives them the strength to grow into monster hurricanes.

A hole in the ozone layer.

Hole in the sky!

High above the Earth, there is a layer of invisible gas called ozone. It protects our skin from the sun's harmful rays. But now scientists have spotted a hole in the ozone layer, and some of those deadly rays are getting through.

Frightful fridges

Some of the villains causing the ozone hole are aerosol cans and refrigerators. Often, these household objects contain chemicals called chlorofluorocarbons, or CFCs. These nasty chemicals escape into the atmosphere and gobble up the ozone that floats there.

27

Hot spots

Several places are in the hot seat when it comes to natural disasters. These hot spots are more likely to be hit than anywhere else in the world. Here's a guide to the danger zones.

Ring of Fire ......

North America

Tornado frenzy
Each year, about 1,000 tornadoes spin across the USA. Most of them happen in the Midwest.

Earthquake zone
The San Andreas Fault is a long stretch of shaky ground along the coast of California, USA. Here, big cities are in the firing line for earthquakes.

Not a drop
The Sahel in Africa is the world's worst area for droughts. For up to three years, this hot, dusty region may have no rain, while rain pours down on lands nearby.

South America

Pacific Ocean

Ring of Fire ......

Key

tornadoes   droughts   volcanoes   floods

earthquakes   hurricanes   icy winds

Ring of Fire

The edge of the Pacific Ocean is an explosive place. Most of the world's active volcanoes lie here in a circle called the Ring of Fire.

Raining again

For up to half a year, the northwest of India may be flooded by rainstorms brought by monsoon winds. For the rest of the year, hardly any rain falls!

Pacific Ocean

Philippine Islands

India

Africa

Blasted shores

The Philippine Islands are the top hurricane hot spot. Each summer, the islands are pounded by hurricanes. When one leaves, often another one arrives.

Ice king

The land around the South Pole, called Antarctica, suffers the worst winter storms. Icy snow blasts along as fast as a speeding car.

Antarctica

Nature's most
wanted

Natural disasters are the world's worst troublemakers. They break all the rules and cause havoc wherever they go. Here are some of the worst offenders.

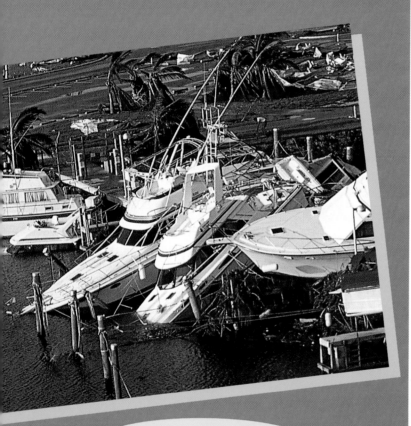

Angry Andrew

Hurricane Andrew was the most expensive natural disaster ever in the USA. One morning, in 1992, its billowing winds tore through Florida, toppling homes and battering yachts. It caused $30 billion (£20 billion) worth of damage. That's the cost of building about 100 Millenium Domes!

Twister gangs

America is never safe from the threat of twisters. In a single month in 1995, a gang of nearly 400 tornadoes terrorized 36 states. An incredible 86 of the twisters appeared in just one day.

Terrible trio

In May 1970, the town of Yungay in Peru was hit three times in a row. First, its resident were shaken out of bed by an earthquake. Next, the town flooded and finally, it was engulfed by a monster mudslide.

Undercover agents

Not all volcanoes are bad guys! Many volcanoes are wanted for their hot properties. Volcanic rocks heat up water underground. In Iceland, this hot water is piped into people's homes, straight into their bathrooms.

Smoke screen

Volcanoes cause record-breaking explosions. They can blow an incredible 50,000 cubic metres of hot ash and rocks into the air. That's enough to fill the Great Pyramid in Egypt 50 times over!

Index